CW01262434

A GUIDE TO LIFE FOR YOUNG MEN AGED 13+

Dave Whitehead

BALBOA.PRESS
A DIVISION OF HAY HOUSE

Copyright © 2020 Dave Whitehead.

All rights reserved. No part of this book may be used or reproduced by any means, graphic, electronic, or mechanical, including photocopying, recording, taping or by any information storage retrieval system without the written permission of the author except in the case of brief quotations embodied in critical articles and reviews.

Balboa Press books may be ordered through booksellers or by contacting:

Balboa Press
A Division of Hay House
1663 Liberty Drive
Bloomington, IN 47403
www.balboapress.co.uk
1 (877) 407-4847

Because of the dynamic nature of the Internet, any web addresses or links contained in this book may have changed since publication and may no longer be valid. The views expressed in this work are solely those of the author and do not necessarily reflect the views of the publisher, and the publisher hereby disclaims any responsibility for them.

The author of this book does not dispense medical advice or prescribe the use of any technique as a form of treatment for physical, emotional, or medical problems without the advice of a physician, either directly or indirectly. The intent of the author is only to offer information of a general nature to help you in your quest for emotional and spiritual well-being. In the event you use any of the information in this book for yourself, which is your constitutional right, the author and the publisher assume no responsibility for your actions.

Any people depicted in stock imagery provided by Getty Images are models, and such images are being used for illustrative purposes only. Certain stock imagery © Getty Images.

Print information available on the last page.

ISBN: 978-1-9822-8136-6 (sc)
ISBN: 978-1-9822-8138-0 (hc)
ISBN: 978-1-9822-8137-3 (e)

Library of Congress Control Number: 2020904068

Balboa Press rev. date: 03/02/2020

CONTENTS

Introduction ix
User Log xi
Amendments xiii

1. Who Are You? 1
2. How Old Are You? 5
3. Home Dynamics 7
4. Friendship 9
5. Courage 11
6. Honesty 13
7. Education 15
8. Technology 19
9. Beauty and Looks 21
10. Possessions 23
11. Ethnicity 25
12. Religion 27
13. You're Normal 29
14. Bullying 31
15. Gangs 33
16. Drugs 35
17. Crime 37
18. Sex 39
19. Abuse 41
20. Applying for a Job 43

21. Finance 47
22. Gambling 49
23. Opportunity 51
24. Loneliness 53
25. Love 55
26. Marriage and Civil Partnerships 59
27. Children 61
28. Separation and Divorce 65
29. Health and Illness 67
30. Society 71
31. Self-Harm 73
32. Suicide 75
33. Bereavement 77
34. Death 79
35. Pets 81
36. Sport 83
37. Finally 89

Dedicated to the good men who shaped my character as a boy and the good women who worked tirelessly to change it when I became a man.

INTRODUCTION

Young human males tend to be reserved about their feelings. They are also patient, tolerant, and happy-go-lucky in their approach to relationships and life in general. This often puts them at a disadvantage when they encounter those who are dynamic and ambitious and who do not consider a laid-back approach as being a positive trait.

The aim of this book is to provide a base upon which boys and young men can consider the many conflicting aspects of life they may face on their journey into manhood.

USER LOG

This page should be used to record the transfer of the book from one person to another. It should include the initial gifting of the book by the purchaser to the first recipient. Names, short messages, and, ideally, current passport-sized photographs should be inserted in the three columns below to create a historical record of the owners of the book.

Date   **From**   **To**

AMENDMENTS

Should the owner deem it necessary to amend or annotate any content of this book, it should be done legibly on the appropriate page. A record of the amendment should then be inserted in the columns below.

Date　　　　　**Page amended**　　　　　**Name**

1
WHO ARE YOU?

The chances are you're not quite sure who you are or haven't given it much thought.

Your character has developed through your experiences as a child. You have been exposed to the influence of your parents or guardians, siblings, grandparents, teachers, and friends.

Be in no doubt that, whether you like it or not, you will have inherited genetically some characteristics of your parents and their parents.

You may also have role models who you wish to emulate who affect your character.

It is important to be yourself. Don't try to be something you're not; it's hard work and not worth the effort. Learn to like yourself. You have many good qualities and some not so good ones. Enhance the good and learn to control those that will let you down.

Try looking at yourself as others see you.

Remember that before you can be true to anyone else, you must learn to be true to yourself.

The poem *Desiderata* by Max Ehrmann (1872–1945), written in the 1920s, may help to guide you in your early years.

Dave Whitehead

Go placidly amid the noise and haste,
and remember what peace there may be in silence.
As far as possible without surrender
be on good terms with all persons.
Speak your truth quietly and clearly;
and listen to others,
even the dull and the ignorant;
they too have their story.

Avoid loud and aggressive persons,
they are vexations to the spirit.
If you compare yourself with others,
you may become vain and bitter;
for always there will be greater and lesser persons than yourself.
Enjoy your achievements as well as your plans.

Keep interested in your own career, however humble;
it is a real possession in the changing fortunes of time.
Exercise caution in your business affairs;
for the world is full of trickery.
But let this not blind you to what virtue there is;
many persons strive for high ideals;
and everywhere life is full of heroism.

Be yourself.
Especially, do not feign affection.
Neither be cynical about love;
for in the face of all aridity and disenchantment
it is as perennial as the grass.

Take kindly the counsel of the years,
gracefully surrendering the things of youth.
Nurture strength of spirit to shield you in sudden misfortune.

But do not distress yourself with dark imaginings.
Many fears are born of fatigue and loneliness.
Beyond a wholesome discipline
be gentle with yourself.

You are a child of the universe,
no less than the trees and the stars;
you have a right to be here.
And whether or not it is clear to you,
no doubt the universe is unfolding as it should.

Therefore be at peace with God,
whatever you conceive Him to be,
and whatever your labors and aspirations,
in the noisy confusion of life keep peace with your soul.
With all its sham, drudgery, and broken dreams,
it is still a beautiful world.
Be cheerful.
Strive to be happy.

2
HOW OLD ARE YOU?

At 13, most boys are interested in computer games, football, bikes, and tropical fish, for example. They might have a passing interest in sex of some sort, which may be viewed with trepidation. Sexual awareness may reveal itself with erections at odd, unexpected occasions.

At 15, most boys will have more than a passing interest in sex due to their physical development. Sexual arousal is a natural phenomenon, which can be very intense at this age.

It is important that you do not allow yourself to be adversely affected by peer pressure. You will not be behind the power curve if you don't have sex when everyone else claims to have done so. Take your time. Find the right partner.

Don't ignore your hobbies; they form an important part of your life and will provide many hours of pleasure and relaxation.

It is important to understand that girls are more mature than boys in their teenage years. A girl may show intense interest in a boy, driven by her instincts to find a mate, but it doesn't mean she is promiscuous or determined to have sex. It is possible that she will be as shy and nervous as the boy she fancies.

Remember that the young girl or boy you fancy is human and has feelings just like you. They can be easily hurt. Treat them with dignity and decency, but don't be a pushover. Stand your ground—and don't give up your tropical fish.

Teenage years are full of new experiences. Your body is changing from a boy to a man. It will be confusing at times. Don't rush through this phase of your life. Take your time, and don't be afraid to talk to those you trust about anything you don't understand. If there is no one, then you must rely on your own judgement. Be honest with yourself. You will sometimes make mistakes, due to inexperience, but they won't be made through carelessness.

William Henry Davies's (1871–1940) poem *Leisure* may help you slow down during this hectic phase of your life.

> What is life if, full of care,
> We have no time to stand and stare.
>
> No time to stand beneath the boughs
> And stare as long as sheep or cows.
>
> No time to see, when woods we pass,
> Where squirrels hide their nuts in grass.
>
> No time to see, in broad daylight,
> Streams full of stars like skies at night.
>
> No time to turn at Beauty's glance,
> And watch her feet, how they can dance.
>
> No time to wait till her mouth can
> Enrich that smile her eyes began.
>
> A poor life this if, full of care,
> We have no time to stand and stare.

3
HOME DYNAMICS

This section deals with family. It is not specifically about a standard family of two parents and one or more children living under the same roof. Nor is it about single-parent families or children's homes. It applies loosely to any group of adults and children living together as a family.

It is intended to describe how to live in a positive, cohesive, and fair way to create and maintain harmony. This will help to develop good social skills and values. It will also provide the foundation when you yourself start your own family and are in a position of responsibility involving children.

In the animal kingdom, when a young male starts to throw his weight around, he is seen off by the senior, stronger leader of the group, often after a violent clash. The young male has no choice but to go away and start his own family. To do this, he must be stronger and tougher than any rivals. This is the way of the animal world, and it promotes natural selection so that the species remains healthy. It occurs instinctively.

To some extent, the same can be said of human families. The head of the family may or may not be physically stronger than you, but they will have more experience of life. They will also have worked to provide the conditions you live in. They may be the only source of income.

It is up to you to support them for the benefit of all members of the family.

If you cannot, it is time to go out and seek your own fortune and create your own family.

It is not right to take on a parasitical role, constantly taking, giving nothing, and at the same time, undermining the authority of the head of the family.

Circumstances can be difficult; however, it is important that you maintain a sensible, dignified, and cheerful dialogue with the head of the family. This will help to create a more enjoyable atmosphere for the whole family and may avoid the sort of confrontation which could lead to your ejection.

4
FRIENDSHIP

What qualities do you require of a friend? (And what does your friend require of you?)

- Loyalty?—Yes.
- Honesty?—Yes.
- Trustworthiness?—Yes.
- Steadfastness in the face of adversity?—Yes.
- Companionship?—Yes, but not necessarily constant.
- Similar interests?—These are not essential, but they can help the friendship evolve.

Throughout our lives, we make many acquaintances who may be loosely regarded as friends. A few of them will become real friends. These people should be treated with kindness, dignity, and understanding. You must go the extra mile for them when they need help.

A true friend is one who gives support without question, one who stands by you when others are critical and when you're going through a tough time.

A true friend will always give you good advice, even when it may be something you don't want to hear.

Do not be drawn into selecting your friends by their looks, fashion sense, sporting prowess, or popularity. These things are not qualities that reflect someone's true character. Look for those who have purity of spirit and inner strength. Look for those who don't always run with the pack.

So the qualities you require of a good friend are, of course, the same as they require of you.

Finally, when you choose a partner for life, in addition to becoming your lover, they should also be your friend (even your best friend).

5

COURAGE

Courage is not being fearless. Courage is the act of overcoming fear.

We aren't all brave in every situation. Some can enjoy hanging by their fingernails on a rock face but have a morbid fear of drowning. Others throw themselves off bridges while tied to an elastic rope but are frightened of the dark. The point is, their courage has many facets.

Courage and fear are not necessarily constant. You may enjoy doing acrobatics on a skateboard whilst you are young but view with trepidation the same thing in your thirties, when you have a family that depends on you.

The most mild-mannered, timid person can turn fierce when protecting loved ones. This is especially true in the case of mothers, in the human race and elsewhere in the animal kingdom.

Fearlessness generated through alcohol or drugs is not courage.

There will be times when you need to be courageous. You will know when that time comes. Do not consider yourself cowardly even though you may be frightened. You were born with the capability for courage. Your body will create the adrenaline (strength and speed) you need, but you will also need presence of mind so that you can concentrate on what needs to be done, rather than what you fear. That is the courage part. When the time comes, do your best. That is all that anyone can ask of you.

The following quotation from Theodore Roosevelt (1858–1919) is inspirational:

> It is not the critic who counts; not the man who points out how the strong man stumbles, or where the doer of deeds could have done them better. The credit belongs to the man who is actually in the arena, whose face is marred by dust and sweat and blood; who strives valiantly; who errs, who comes short again and again, because there is no effort without error and shortcoming; but who does actually strive to do the deeds; who knows great enthusiasms, the great devotions; who spends himself in a worthy cause; who at the best knows in the end the triumph of high achievement, and who at the worst, if he fails, at least fails while daring greatly, so that his place shall never be with those cold and timid souls who neither know victory nor defeat.

6

HONESTY

It is hard to be honest all the time. For example, we are often encouraged to tell white lies when we are part of a conspiracy to give someone a pleasant surprise on their birthday.

Totally unrestricted honesty tends to make one unpopular and regarded by others as blunt, rude, or abrasive. We learn as we grow older to be diplomatic, when honesty may cause distress or offence. Whilst this trait may be regarded as not lying, it clearly cannot be regarded as entirely truthful either.

Lying to avoid being chastised or punished for a misdemeanour or crime may get you off the hook initially, but the lie will invariably be harder to maintain, and the truth will be discovered eventually. This will do nothing for your reputation or self-esteem. You may also lose friends and the respect of others as a result.

Making false statements on documents or contracts, lying to the police when under caution, and lying under oath in a court of law can land you in deep trouble.

Honesty requires courage. Don't let yourself down by taking the easy way out, when confronted about something you have or haven't done.

Perhaps the worst thing about lying is that you will be dissatisfied with your own weakness, causing your own self-respect to suffer.

The following quote from the play *Marmion* by Sir Walter Scott (1771–1832) sums it up: "Oh! What a tangled web we weave when first we practise to deceive!"

7

EDUCATION

Education systems are not perfect. The main reason is the way in which all children are categorised by age to fit into a school curriculum. No two children are the same. Some develop faster than others. Some are gifted mathematically, whilst others are good at literacy; additionally, some have good long-term memories, but others can't remember anything they read the previous day. Some of us are clumsy; others are gifted with hand and eye skills, such as art and crafts. There are those who can produce outstanding technical drawings but are unable to create an artistic picture.

The point is that none of us are good at everything, but everyone is good at something. It is important that you learn what skills you have and, just as important, what skills you don't have.

It is critical that you are able to read, write, and understand arithmetic before you leave school. Most shortcomings in these subjects can be overcome with additional study; however, you will need to tell your teachers/tutors/parents as soon as you become aware that you are experiencing difficulties so they can take timely action to help you before you fall so far behind your classmates it becomes very difficult to catch up. Do not be afraid to do so for fear of ridicule by your peers; this is your life, your future.

There are modern ways of dealing with dyslexia and similar difficulties that will be of considerable benefit should you be challenged by such conditions.

If it becomes necessary to move you to a lower grade of class, grasp the opportunity. Learning will be much easier, and you will be more content at the end of the school day. You will also have a better chance of gaining useful qualifications.

Further education provides an opportunity for you to enhance the qualifications you have already achieved. You can also specialize in subjects you need for future employment. This can include technical, craft, and industrial courses. Do not give up the opportunity further education offers. You may feel that you have spent enough of your life in classrooms; however, when you go job hunting, you will be competing with many others the same age as you and older people too who have previous experience in the workplace. Therefore, take full advantage of every chance to increase your knowledge.

University is possible if you get sufficiently good grades. Bear in mind that you will compete with others to gain a place at university, so you will need to work very hard to get a place on the degree course you want at the place you want. Failure to get a place at university doesn't make you a failure. You will have many qualities and skills to offer. Look for another route to employment, such as apprenticeships and even self-employment.

So you've left school. You may have responsibilities or not, in which case, you're very lucky; at that time, you are in the unique position of being able to take calculated risks, without it adversely affecting anyone else. Don't wait until you have a partner, children, a mortgage, a dog, and a car to decide you want to go backpacking around the world; do it now. If you want to climb Everest, do it now. If you want to help villagers in remote areas of Chile, do it now. You will discover much about yourself, meet a wide variety of good people, and broaden your outlook.

You may find that special someone, special place, or special job at the same time. Don't wait until you're sixty and wish you'd done it. Employers are looking for that extra experience when looking for new blood. Who knows? The life experience you gained after you left school may make the difference between getting the job you want and not getting it. It all starts at school. Work hard.

8
TECHNOLOGY

Technology offers incredible opportunities in many aspects of life. To take advantage of all the things it can do, you must keep up to date with its applications. There are also many disadvantages to technology, pitfalls that can have an adverse effect on your friendships, reputation, and livelihood.

It must be understood that a computer, and this includes mobile phones, records everything you input and save or send. Deleting will not remove it from the computer or phone. Deleting just moves it to another part of the system memory. Bearing this in mind, you must be careful not to have anything on your system that you wouldn't want your parents, partner, children, or the police to see, at the time or indeed in years to come. The following tips should help you safely use technology:

Use a password and don't let anyone else know it. This will prevent others using your system and ensure your system stays clean.

Don't view any site that breaks the law, such as extremist, racist, or child pornography. Don't get into dialogue with anyone who advocates such things.

Don't make threats through a computer or cell phone, and don't encourage anyone else to do so.

Don't get involved in cyber bullying. It is a disgraceful and cowardly act of intimidation. If it happens to you at school, don't respond; report it to your teacher. If it happens at any other time, don't respond; inform your parents, who will know what action to take, which may involve the police.

Some people will try to groom you on the internet, to create the opportunity to get you alone. They will do so to exploit your trust, innocence, and vulnerability. Invariably, their plan will be to sexually exploit you. Don't agree to meet anyone you have met online, unless you have arranged for your own protection at the rendezvous. Confide in your parents so they can advise you about the perils. If you decide to meet someone you've never met before, take a trusted friend with you. Ideally, when you are young, this should be an adult. Be careful.

Don't take, send, or store photos of a sexual nature, of yourself or anyone else; they can easily end up on websites and social networks all over the world. As with many aspects of technology, they can come back to haunt you, at critical times in your life, such as when you are in a high-profile professional appointment, or if you are a well-known personality, or about to marry, for example. There are plenty of people out there who will take great delight in ruining you.

Protect personal information on your system, to prevent hackers stealing your identity and, subsequently, your money.

Consider carefully how you ultimately dispose of your system. Remember, everything will be on your hard drive until it is destroyed.

Technology is a very useful tool, but you must be aware of the risks it poses if you use it irresponsibly.

9
BEAUTY AND LOOKS

Beauty is in the eye of the beholder, the saying goes, and it is true. We all have different views about beauty in relation to art, cars, clothes, houses, and, of course, people.

A beautiful exterior does not necessarily mean a beautiful interior. Indeed, it may conceal an ugly interior.

In people, try to look for the beauty inside. Instinct may draw you to well-dressed, well-manicured, well-bred, witty, and clever people, but do they have inner beauty? Do they have a natural affinity towards others, regardless of social standing? Do they tolerate human frailty? Do they show warmth and compassion towards others?

Nobody stays outwardly beautiful for ever. A beautiful mind and spirit will outlive a beautiful countenance. So look for that special, unique person. To you, they will always be beautiful, regardless of the ravages of time.

You should, of course, consider whether you too have that special quality, special enough to make such a person want to be your friend.

Choose well. Time spent doing so will not be wasted. This quotation by Robert Burns (1759–1796) is thought-provoking: "Oh would some power the giftie gie us, to see ourselves as others see us."

10

POSSESSIONS

Many are distracted from the important things in life by the perceived need to accumulate valuable possessions. This can cause us to envy others who have more possessions than we do.

Perhaps the only valuable physical possessions have sentimental value, such as an heirloom, handed down by someone we love, or something given by someone special, or some award we've been given. Such possessions are things we will want to pass to someone special when the time is right.

Other possessions, such as your home or apartment, car or truck, furniture, and clothes, are merely tools that enable us to live comfortably and should be regarded as such. They should not be regarded as status symbols. We should not waste effort accumulating these tools because, as we get older, they'll become less important to us, and we'll come to understand that our time could have been better spent gathering more important things.

The pleasure you experience from knowing you have the love of your family, and the admiration and respect of your friends and colleagues, will far outweigh the pleasure you get from owning a fast car or a piece of land. These possessions are worthy of your time and efforts, and they can bring you much happiness throughout your life.

11

ETHNICITY

It is right to be proud of your roots. You should also acknowledge the right of other people to be proud of their roots.

Nations have been conquered, colonised, and governed by other nations since the beginning of civilisation. Countries have fought one another and fought for one another. They have changed their borders, had their borders changed for them, and separated into one or more countries after treaties.

The chances of our own bloodlines being traced back to the beginning of civilisation, without the introduction of a different tribe, is at best remote.

The major wars of the past created conditions where people of all nationalities, colours, and religions fought side by side to rid the world of tyrannical and corrupt regimes that offered nothing but hatred and bigotry. It is therefore right that our generation should ensure there is no hatred or bigotry in our world that so many good people fought and died to establish.

Do not judge people by their appearance. All of us are capable of good and bad things. Get to know people before you form an opinion of them. Do not form an opinion based on the views of others. Be your own man.

Have a sense of fair play and equality in your dealings with others. You will not gain the respect of others if you are inconsistent in how you treat them.

Remember that promoting racial or religious hatred is a crime in many countries. Having a conviction for doing so will almost certainly affect your future livelihood.

Treat everyone as equals.

12

RELIGION

Religion can be a very emotional subject. Religious wars and other crises have taken place throughout the world since the beginning of civilisation. They will continue to occur in the future.

Most religious writings prescribe rules that encourage communities to live in harmony.

Sadly, religious fervour can develop into fanaticism. This is often due to religious texts being interpreted and taught in a way that supports those who use them to justify their own bigoted beliefs.

In many cases, sects within the same religion distrust one another. This often causes bigotry, hatred, and fear.

Try not to get drawn into groups where religious fervour demands that you adopt extremist views. It could cause disruption in your life and may be illegal too.

Whether you are religion or agnostic, it is important that you develop these traits: honesty, tolerance, respect, and compassion for others.

By doing so, you will gain the friendship and trust of those who know you. It will take time and effort. It will not happen just because you think you're a good person. The poem by Sir Henry

Dave Whitehead

Wotton (1568–1639), *The Character of a Happy Life*, follows for your consideration.

> How happy is he born and taught,
> That serveth not another's will;
> Whose Armour is his honest thought,
> And simple truth his utmost skill;
>
> Whose passions not his Masters are;
> Whose Soul is still prepar'd for Death,
> Unti'd unto the World by care
> Of public Fame, or private Breath;
> Who envies none that chance doth raise,
> Or vice; who never understood
> How deepest Wounds are given by praise;
> Not rules of State, but Rules of good;
>
> Who hath his Life from Rumours freed;
> Whose Conscience is his strong retreat;
> Whose State can neither Flatterers feed,
> Nor Ruin make Oppressors great;
>
> Who God doth late and early pray
> More of his Grace than Gifts to lend;
> And entertains the harmless day
> With a Religious book or friend!
>
> This man is freed from servile bands
> Of hope to rise, or fear to fall:
> Lord of himself, though not of lands;
> And having nothing, yet hath all.

13

YOU'RE NORMAL

Fat, thin, tall, short, black, white, or brown: All are normal. Don't let your perception about your appearance hold you back.

Old, young, spotty, not spotty, clever, not clever: All are normal. You are unique. Be proud of who you are.

Rich, poor, talented, or not, you're normal. Do the best you can.

Liked, not liked, loved, not loved, alone: You're normal. Be strong in isolation; it won't last for long.

Weak, strong, confident or not, you're normal. Good people will recognise a good heart and soul.

Disabled, or ill, or a victim of your birth, you're normal. Don't look back. You're special. Move on.

Heterosexual, bisexual, homosexual, transsexual: You're normal. Sex without love is just sex. Sex between two people who love each other is wonderful.

Being truthful, honourable, and pure of spirit is not so normal. We all try to be but generally fail; that's normal. Do the best you can, and try not to hurt anyone.

You have a purpose. Find out what it is. Having found it, pursue it. That's normal.

Most of us live normal lives. Give your love to those who need it. Giving is normal.

It's not normal for people to enjoy spoiling your dreams and aspirations. They may have weaknesses of their own to conceal. Be strong; don't doubt yourself. Cling to your dreams; that's normal.

Don't categorize or stigmatize yourself. You're normal. So live life to the full. Don't waste time. Time is not on your side.

14

BULLYING

Bullying is an extremely unpleasant form of behaviour, evident mainly in schools and the workplace.

In the animal kingdom, the fittest, strongest, and most aggressive creatures take what they want from weaker animals, who submit by cowering or running away.

In the undeveloped world, where life and livelihood depend on good health, strength, and ability, the strongest will invariably be first in the queue for food.

Whilst there is a good reason for such behaviour among animals and in the undeveloped world, there is no excuse for it in modern society.

People sometimes become bullies because they were bullied themselves. A group of bullies usually comprises one particularly nasty person, who leads a group of weak and cowardly characters. These individuals enjoy the power they feel when they frighten or intimidate gentle, fair-minded, and decent people. Bullies will try to isolate an individual they want to intimidate. It is important that friends, colleagues, and workmates support people who are the subject of bullying. This should be done without the use of force, unless there is a clear and present danger to their safety.

You may find examples of bullying in all walks of life, commencing when you start school. Do not be surprised by it.

Learn to deal with it as constructively and positively as possible, without resorting to bullying yourself. This will take courage and tact. Most educational, commercial, social, and sporting organisations have procedures in place for dealing with bullying. Find out what they are, and don't be frightened to use them.

If you are reading this and you are a bully, you can change. With that change will come self-respect and better friends. It will not be easy, because you will have to break away from your group of bullies, but it will be worth it in the end.

15

GANGS

A group of friends who meet regularly to hang out together is not a gang.

A group drawn together for strength in numbers, to do things which are criminal, unsociable, or immoral, is a gang.

Such gangs are a sad element of modern society. They generally exist in deprived neighbourhoods in cities and large towns.

It may be difficult to avoid joining a gang in your local area, where they have developed into regimented hierarchies. Gangs usually have initiation rites that require you to break the law in some way to demonstrate your worthiness to be a member. Gangs may also be subordinate to adult criminals, which will considerably increase the chances of your involvement in serious criminal activity.

You must do all you can to avoid being drawn into any gang that regards itself as outside the law. If you cannot avoid it, it could ruin any chance you have of a decent life.

If necessary, you may have to consider leaving the area to seek your fortune elsewhere. It would help if you could live with a relative or good friend well away from the gang's influence. Joining the Navy, Army, or Air Force might be the answer. Discuss options with a close relative you can trust; do not under any circumstances discuss it with gang members or their associates.

If you get into trouble as a result of your activities as a gang member, you will have a record. That record can be seen by any organisation vetting you for employment. This will automatically rule you out of many job opportunities. In situations where there are hundreds of applications for one job, the employer will want to see evidence of honesty, reliability, and strength of character. Having a record will almost certainly mean your application doesn't go any further.

Best advice, therefore, is to stay away from gangs.

16

DRUGS

Drugs come in many forms. Medicinal drugs are designed to remedy health problems, but recreational drugs are not good for you. It is the latter that is dealt with in this section.

Drugs invariably change your mood and personality whilst you are under their influence.

The sale of tobacco and alcohol is generally well-regulated. Whilst not completely safe to use, they are manufactured from legal, well-managed sources. Illegal drugs, by their very nature, have no guarantee of safety, are virtually untraceable, and therefore they represent a high risk to users.

Smoking tobacco may make you feel calm when you're under stress, but it frequently causes severe health problems later in life. It is a known killer, and the period leading up to death by lung cancer is normally extremely traumatic.

Consuming alcohol can relax you and may make you exceptionally good-humoured. It may also make you confrontational and aggressive. The more alcohol you drink, the less inhibited you will become. Drunkenness can put you in serious trouble with the law, put your life in danger, or at the very least cause you embarrassment. Alcohol is a killer. As with smoking, the period leading up to death from liver problems is extremely painful.

Using drugs such as cannabis, opiates, and cocaine will give you a feeling of well-being, but you may be in danger of becoming dependent on them. This will adversely impact on your health and can cause your death. It will also have a considerable impact on your financial situation. Many addicts resort to extreme measures such as stealing and selling themselves for sex to fund their habit.

Taking drugs used at raves or parties to give make you high can be extremely dangerous. They frequently cause death because of the damage they do to vital body organs.

It might seem a good idea to try some form of drug to demonstrate to your friends that you are one of the crowd and not frightened of authority. If you do, the risks you face will far outweigh the short-lived kudos you experience at the time.

Good friends don't encourage each other to take drugs.

It is easy to start using illegal drugs. It is considerably difficult to stop. Save your money, and who knows; you may save your own life.

17

CRIME

Sadly, many young people get drawn into criminal activity, either of their own volition or because their personal circumstances leave them little choice. Whatever the reason behind it, in a life of crime, there are no winners. The criminals, their families, the victims, and society all pay in the end.

Government and commercial agencies maintain databases of digital information. Many cooperate with each other, exchanging information on a routine basis.

Personal and financial details, purchasing habits, and technology use are all recorded somewhere. Most importantly, anything anyone does which comes under law or security services scrutiny will also be recorded. The point is, there isn't much we do that isn't visible in some way.

Many employers now seek this information while vetting potential employees. Some jobs require a check to see if you have a police record of any kind. A police caution may not be formalised into a charge and subsequent court appearance, but it will be held on record and show up on any subsequent vetting checks.

A caution for a minor offence may not be considered serious to a future employer; however, in an environment where many apply for one job, that could be the reason your application goes no further.

Being imprisoned is an awful experience for anyone. It will do nothing positive for your future. Indeed, it could ruin your entire life. To come through such an experience, rebuild a life, and start a career requires strength of character, ability, and not a little good fortune.

You should also consider the effect that criminal activity has on family members and others close to them. They may give considerable support following your arrest and subsequent trial. They may continue that support while you're imprisoned and after your release. Nevertheless, they will feel badly let down but will make many sacrifices to give you that support.

After prison, you must do your best to recover your integrity, rebuild your reputation, and repay those who gave such unstinting support.

As you get older, you may take on responsibility for others, which requires you to live as a decent, honest member of society. Doing so will give you more satisfaction than criminal activities. It will also mean that you will associate with like-minded people.

So avoiding conflict with the law is something to take very seriously indeed.

18

SEX

Sex is likely to be the most confusing, frustrating, and worrying aspect of being a teenager. Indeed, such issues may continue well into adulthood.

Sex education is generally delivered at various stages of schooling. This may take several forms but may not do much to clarify your thoughts on the subject. The instruction may also be more clinical than emotional in its approach.

Young male teenagers are normally affected by puberty, a time of dynamic physical changes. This is a time when hair starts to grow on the face, under the arms, and around the penis and testicles. They also become more sexually aware, both consciously and unconsciously. They take more interest in their own physical appearance and those of others, finding themselves attracted to some of them. This may cause them to experience an erection. Sometimes, they may awake with an erection. These things are natural human processes and are nothing to be ashamed of. Nor should they cause concern.

An erection can sometimes lead to an ejaculation of sperm. This causes an intensely enjoyable sensation but can be a bit messy. This experience should not be shared publicly. There's no need to feel ashamed or dirty afterwards. This is an important part of the learning process in discovering how genitals function.

Masturbation, that is the action to bring about an ejaculation unaided, is natural and nothing to be self-critical about.

The best way to enjoy sex is to do it with someone else, someone you like a lot and who feels the same way you do. Nervousness, shyness, and embarrassment will be more easily overcome with someone you like. It is important to help one another to avoid discomfort (inexperience may lead to pain during penetration).

It is sensible to use a condom. It will help in the lubrication process during intercourse; dryness can cause discomfort. A condom will prevent pregnancy. Unless you are planning to be a father, wear a condom. The financial burden for fathering a child is considerable, regardless of whether you remain with the mother or not. A condom can help avoid sexually transmitted diseases. Passing on a sexually transmitted disease to another is disgraceful and a betrayal of trust. When you have sex, it is your responsibility to ensure that both you and your partner are protected.

Finally, there is no greater experience than having sex with someone you love who loves you too. Love is the ingredient that enhances all other sexual feelings and activities. Don't rush into having sex because you feel pressured by your friends. Time is on your side; find that special soulmate. After that, all other things become possible, and life really does begin.

19

ABUSE

There is no doubt that being abused will change your life. It can cause pain and anguish. It disrupts your natural emotional development, leading to relationship problems for the remaining childhood years and later in adulthood too. Under law, a child under 16 is not considered mature enough to know right from wrong. Additionally, children are generally unable to protect themselves. The abuse of a child, therefore, is a disgraceful and shameful act. It is against the law and carries severe penalties.

If you experience physical, sexual, or emotional abuse, there are several options available to you:

- Go to the nearest police station and tell them about it.
- Tell your parents or guardians, if you can.
- Contact your local council children's services department (find their contact details on the internet).
- Contact a children's charity helpline, such as the Royal Society for the Protection of Children.
- Tell your doctor, nurse, or teacher.
- Tell your youth or sports club leader.

All these groups have policies and procedures that require them to take action in response to what you tell them. It may seem a lengthy process, but don't give up.

You may not be the only one who is being abused by the same person. So you may also be helping others by reporting the matter.

It's also important to remember that the abuse is not your fault.

20
APPLYING FOR A JOB

There are two important stages to consider when applying for a job. The first is the application itself, which will include your personal details, qualifications, background, and experience. The second, assuming your application is successful, is the interview, where your suitability will be assessed by your answers to questions.

Dealing with your application first, do some research to find out the following:

- Is it a job you really want to do?
- Is it a reputable company?
- Does the job description match your capabilities?
- Are the pay and conditions acceptable?
- Is there a pension plan? (If not, the employer is not complying with the law.)
- Will your transportation costs be reasonable?

When writing your application, keep asking yourself what the employer is looking for. The following points are useful:

- Ensure the application is relevant to the job. It won't help if you write in detail about your apprenticeship as a butcher when you're applying for a clerical post (unless, of course, the job is for a butcher).

- Include details of any youth qualifications or memberships such as the Scouts. Adventurous pursuits, sports, charitable work, and hobbies will also give the employer an insight into your character. This will demonstrate that you are independent, outgoing, and a team player.
- Don't bluff; you will be caught out if you get an interview.
- Ask anyone you intend to nominate for a reference before you include them in your application. At the time you ask them, you will have the opportunity to request that they specify any qualities you have which will emphasise your suitability for the job.
- Write out a rough draft of your application before committing yourself to writing. An untidy, poorly spelt application with corrections and creases is likely to be discarded before it is read.
- Show your draft to someone with experience. They may note some glaring errors or give you some useful tips.
- Use a good pen that won't smudge or run out midapplication.
- If a curriculum vitae is required, tailor it to the job. Don't use the same CV for every application (unless you are applying to similar jobs).

If you are invited for an interview, review again the job description and any information you've found about the company. Time spent in preparation is seldom wasted.

- Allow yourself adequate time to prepare. Don't leave it until the last minute.
- Be ready to tell them something about yourself, which is commonly used as an icebreaker. They will have read your application but want to see your character.

- Research the company because you will almost certainly be asked what you know about its reputation, activities, and so on.
- Research the job description again to ensure you are ready to answer questions about your ability to do it.
- Consider what to wear. Most job interviews should be attended wearing jacket and tie. Some may require a suit. Smart casual clothes may be better for some. It is important that you give the right impression.
- The interviewer will probably ask why you want the job. It is important that you display enthusiasm. Your research should have highlighted opportunities for advancement and the chance to gain more qualifications.
- The interviewer will ask about your strengths and weaknesses. (We all have them; it is a good human quality to recognise them in ourselves so we can manage them in a way society expects). For example, a friendly, good-humoured, easy-going person may be ideally suited as a travel rep but would not be a very effective prison officer. Being someone who sticks rigidly to rules, precisely and obstinately, may be a nightmare in the hospitality sector but would be ideal in a trade where noncompliance could cause an accident. Therefore, apply your strengths and weaknesses to the job you are being interviewed for.
- You may be asked what your priorities would be if you get the job. Your research and considerations about the job should provide the answer. Would you want to get to know the team you're working with? Would you want to familiarise yourself with the workplace and equipment? Prepare a well-rehearsed but natural-sounding answer for these questions.

- You will be asked when you'd be able to start. Don't put any obstacles in the way. If you do, you may not get the job.
- Don't expect high wages straight away. Getting a job is difficult. It is easier to get promotion and to network with other work colleagues and business associates to gain advancement once you're in a job.

Finally, working for cash in hand leads to a black economy. It is illegal because your employer and you are defrauding other taxpayers. It also means that you and your employer are not contributing towards your pension, which is also against the law. Additionally, your pension when you reach old age is going to be lower as a result.

Don't give up trying to get a job. Take every training opportunity available to you. It will pay off in the end.

21

FINANCE

It is very easy to get credit. It is seldom easy to repay it. If you're hard up and lose your income, through illness or by becoming unemployed, interest rates will continue to grow. Being heavily in debt can ruin your life, your livelihood, and your relationships too.

It is worth considering the following points to enable you to be financially prudent:

- There is an old saying, "A fool and his money are soon parted." It is very true. Don't spend your hard-earned cash to impress your friends. If they are real friends, you won't need to.
- Don't buy anything you don't need. When you do, choose the most economical model that suits your need; don't go for the flashiest, most expensive item to impress others.
- If you must use credit, do it through a reputable organisation such as a bank or a reputable credit card provider. Don't use instant loan companies (loan sharks).
- Don't overdraw on your normal bank account. The interest rates are generally higher than arranged loans, and if you do it regularly, your credit rating will suffer.

- Regularly reconcile your bank statement with your records of expenditure. It will provide you with useful statistics about your way of life and will give you the opportunity to consider your spending trends in the future.
- If you are lucky enough to have money to spare, invest it wisely. If you have savings that pay an annual interest of 1 percent but the annual inflation (cost of living) rate is 2 percent, your savings are getting smaller in real terms. A solution could be investment in the stock market. A reputable broker can offer a portfolio of companies with varying degrees of financial risk. The dividends are generally higher than the interest rates set by the banks and building societies.
- Property can be a good long-term investment, but beware of negative equity. This occurs when the property you have bought through a loan falls in value (due to a recession, for example). The money you still owe the finance company may then exceed the value of the property itself. Selling the property will not cover the cost of repaying the loan.

It is crucial to understand the importance that money will have now and throughout your life. Time spent on financial considerations will never be wasted. Start while you're young; it's for your future.

22

GAMBLING

The old saying, "A fool and his money are soon parted", can be applied appropriately to anyone who becomes a compulsive gambler.

Whilst gambling may initially be regarded as good fun, these negative effects are associated with problem gambling:

- Severe financial difficulties, including increasing debt and poverty for gamblers and their dependents; bankruptcy; the loss of credit-worthiness, perhaps indefinitely; and the loss of possessions such as home, car, and other valuable assets.
- Damage to one's reputation caused by borrowing money from family members and friends without paying it back.
- Disruption to family cohesion leading to child abuse, domestic violence, and child behaviour problems.
- Loss of self-esteem.
- Stealing from family, friends, colleagues, or the workplace.
- Involvement in criminal activity to alleviate financial problems.
- Deteriorating health and lack of sleep caused by worry.
- Suicidal tendencies.

It is not just the gambler who suffers when gambling becomes compulsive; those close to them suffer too. Therefore:

- Never gamble with money you can't afford to lose.
- Don't view gambling as a way of making money. Try to see it as entertainment. A small amount now and then on the national lottery or the football cup final won't hurt you financially and will provide a bit of fun.
- Don't get involved in regular games with your friends or anyone else where the stakes are high.
- Don't gamble on the internet; you'll never beat a computer.
- Don't chase your losses by gambling more heavily. You will only slip deeper into debt.

Compulsive gambling is a very quick way to ruin your life and the lives of those around you. Best advice is to never start.

23

OPPORTUNITY

Throughout your life, opportunities will present themselves. Some will be obvious; others will not be. Later in life, many look back and wonder about opportunities they didn't take.

Try to recognise these opportunities when they occur because they might require you to make quick decisions.

Career opportunities are normally straightforward, with time to weigh your options. Financial opportunities must be considered very carefully to ensure you don't end up financially worse off. Opportunities in affairs of the heart are never clear or straightforward and can cause considerable stress and heartache.

Treat all opportunities with honesty (to yourself and others), strength of character, and courage (if necessary).

In matters of the heart, opportunities should be handled with dignity and care; they should not be ignored. You may wonder if a certain someone returns your affection; this question, left unanswered, will not go away. How you ask the question is crucial, but don't be put off. Who knows? You may be lucky.

If you're not lucky, accept it with grace and bear no ill will. Be satisfied that you acted sincerely and in good faith. Then let the matter rest, once and for all.

The poem *"To the Virgin, to Make Much of Time"* by Robert Herrick (1591–1674) gives food for thought.

Gather ye rose-buds while ye may,
Old Time is still a flying;
And this same flow'r, that smiles to-day,
To-morrow will be dying.

The glorious lamp of heav'n, the sun,
The highest he's a getting;
The sooner will his race be run,
And nearer he's to setting.

That age is best which is the first,
When youth and blood are warmer;
But, being spent, the worse; and worst
Times still succeed the former.

Then be not coy, but use your time;
And while ye may, go marry:
For, having lost but once your prime,
You may for ever tarry.

24

LONELINESS

The feeling of loneliness is something we all experience from time to time. Depending on your social and domestic lifestyle, it can last for short or long periods.

Generally, we all enjoy the company of others, and modern electronic devices keep us in touch more than ever before. We are not normally used to being on our own, not talking to anyone for hours. Also, some of us do not have loved ones or friends we can look forward to seeing during our day.

You personally may feel isolated at times, but there are ways you can reduce the feeling of loneliness.

You will not overcome isolation by remaining in your home. You must make a determined effort to get out and meet others.

Sporting, hobby, and social clubs are good ways to meet like-minded people. Long-term friendships can be, and often are, created through such organisations.

The workplace can create opportunities for friendship; it can also open doors to a new job.

Charities are always looking for volunteers. Doing something worthwhile for others will make you feel good; you'll also meet other good people.

Don't try to solve your loneliness by going online. There are some degenerate predators using the internet, who will prey on you without the slightest bit of remorse. So be careful making friends on social media sites. They may be easy to talk to, but you have no guarantee regarding their trustworthiness. They could be genuine young people of your age. They could just as easily be elaborate middle-aged hoaxers, paedophiles grooming you for their own sexual perversion, or criminals, intent on defrauding you. You could be putting yourself in danger.

Being on your own is not always a bad thing. It creates time for you to pursue activities which are best done alone, such as photography, model making, writing, or stamp collecting, to name but a few.

Finally, there may be a special person out there in the world who is also lonely. You are unlikely to ever meet them if you don't get out of the house and put yourself about.

25

LOVE

Love is a very powerful emotion. People experience it many times in some form during their lifetime. You can love your parents, a pet, and chocolate. Later in life, you will love your partner, your children, or even your car.

We all need love. It is the most significant factor in all our lives.

Love is stronger than hate, stronger than ambition, stronger than good or bad. Love will undermine the most carefully made plans, will disrupt convention, and will overcome, or seek to overcome, all attempts to limit or confine it.

Love comes in different intensities. It is unlikely that you will love chocolate as much as your children or your country. Love is seldom consistent. It evolves as your relationship with the object of your love evolves. It is even possible to fall out of love and back in love again, with the same person, as a result of the many changes that naturally occur in a relationship.

When you fall in love, you form a deep relationship with someone else.

Sexual activity may develop during the relationship. It is also possible that love may develop during a sexual relationship. One doesn't necessarily follow the other.

True, deep love does not require sexual activity to be sustained; however, if there is genuine love between two people, sex should not be embarrassing or uncomfortable, because there will be a genuine desire, by both, to please each other in a gentle, considerate, and loving way.

Sex should not be used to prove one's love for another. Love is too important to be used to coerce someone to submit to sexual activity.

Complacency is a great threat to a relationship. Never take love for granted. It must be nurtured and demonstrated, through unselfishness, thoughtfulness, and consideration of one another's needs and feelings. You will want to feel needed, valued, and desired; they will too. You must both ensure it happens.

Love will help you endure difficult, occasionally very hard times. Love will give you strength.

Love should not diminish after you go bald, put on weight, develop an illness, or grow old. If there is real love, such conditions will be managed in the same spirit as all the other difficulties you both faced in the past.

If you're lucky and your love for each other has increased, you will still be together in old age, still holding hands when shopping, still cuddling, still sharing precious moments. That is what love can do for you, if you give it a chance and keep it at the top of your to-do list.

The following writings by D. H. Lawrence (1885–1930) and William Shakespeare (1564–1616) are of interest.

> No form of love is wrong, so long as it is love, and you yourself honour what you are doing. Love has an extraordinary variety of forms! And that is all there is in life, it seems to me.
>
> —D. H. Lawrence

Sonnet 116

Let me not to the marriage of true minds
Admit impediments; love is not love
Which alters when it alteration finds,
Or bends with the remover to remove.
O no, it is an ever-fixèd mark
That looks on tempests and is never shaken;
It is the star to every wandering bark,
Whose worth's unknown, although his height be taken.
Love's not Time's fool, though rosy lips and cheeks
Within his bending sickle's compass come;
Love alters not with his brief hours and weeks,
But bears it out even to the edge of doom.
If this be error and upon me proved,
I never writ, nor no man ever loved.

—William Shakespeare

26

MARRIAGE AND CIVIL PARTNERSHIPS

Before you can be true to another person, you must learn to be true to yourself.

When considering a long-term relationship, such as marriage or civil partnership, it is important to analyse your own feelings honestly, to ensure you are not undertaking something lightly. It is better not to enter into a commitment, in the early stages of a relationship, rather than pull out of it after your partner is convinced of your long-term intentions.

Sometimes, close relatives and friends may create a momentum towards betrothal that is difficult for you to control. What others want or expect is not as important as your future happiness. Therefore, keep a cool head, and don't allow yourself to be pushed against your will.

Marital commitment is not just an expression of love. It is also an expression of trust. Betrayal will cause considerable emotional turmoil. So don't make a promise to someone unless you are completely sure that it is what you want.

If your marriage or civil partnership fails, it is important to understand the following factors:

- Laws differ from country to country in the case of a civil partnership breaking up. Such laws may not make financial provision for either partner.
- In the case of a marriage breaking up, the divorce proceedings will ensure fair play in respect of the division of assets.
- It is worth bearing in mind that as far as the law is concerned, all assets obtained during the marriage have been achieved through the joint efforts of both the husband and wife, even if only one was employed outside the home.
- The courts will also ensure adequate financial provision for the care and maintenance of any children. This will continue for as long as they remain in full-time education; it will have a considerable impact on your finances, life in general, and social activities.

Many marital relationships do go on to be successful. All relationships have their ups and downs. True love will endure the hard times.

27

CHILDREN

It is a sad fact of life that many children are born into conditions that are difficult if not downright appalling. Whilst hunger, disease, and other physical hardships are bad enough, nothing has a worse effect on a child's development than being unloved, unwanted, or abused.

You as a father can and will have a profound effect on your children (I include stepchildren and foster children). As such, it is of the utmost importance that you understand and accept your responsibility to them.

Instinct is all that young children have to protect themselves, and though we may not trust our instincts after we get older, they are very acute in young children.

Do not think that children are too young to understand the environment they live in. Instinct will enable even a newborn baby to detect negative emotions such as anger, impatience, and frustration. Therefore, it's important that you do not convey such things to a child in your care.

Babies cry for a variety of reasons. It is their only way of communicating their distress.

- Hunger and discomfort due to a soiled nappy are common conditions and are easily remedied.

- Tiredness can also cause a baby to cry in what might be perceived as a fit of temper. Far from it, children just need rocking, cuddling, and words of comfort until they settle down and drift off.
- In the early weeks, feeding is often followed by wind, which causes discomfort until it is gently eased.
- Teething in later months will be very painful and can be eased through a variety of readily available medicines.

It is up to you to identify what is causing the distress. You are the adult. It is your responsibility to sooth the baby using whatever means is necessary and in doing so demonstrate calmness, gentleness, and understanding. This will do much to reassure children and help them to settle down.

It is worth remembering that crying itself is not harmful for a baby, so long as it is not persistent. With patience and understanding, you will become experienced at identifying the source of your baby's distress.

Do not allow yourself to become frustrated with yourself if you can't stop a baby crying quickly. Use softly spoken words of comfort and gentle handling whilst you identify the problem.

As babies develop, they will try new things and investigate everything around them. This is how we all learn. You must be constantly alert when a baby is in your charge, to prevent the possibility of injury by things adults and older children regard as everyday items. Falling asleep when looking after a baby who has learnt to crawl is not wise.

When children are disobedient, bad-tempered, or generally naughty, find a way of punishing them without resorting to violence. In such cases, firmness with threats to restrict treats, for example, will produce the desired effect. It is crucial that children learn to behave in the manner you require. Therefore, don't wait until they are three years old before trying to teach them to respond to your instructions properly. It will probably be too late.

If it ever gets to the stage where you are at your wits' end, trying to get a baby settled, seek help and advice from another parent, if necessary. Never let the situation get to the point where you lose your temper and are in danger of hurting the child.

Young children are easily managed using all your love, patience, and understanding. It will not be easy, but it will be tremendously worthwhile and a source of great satisfaction. As a father, you have a great responsibility. Shirk it, and you will never quite forgive yourself, for your failure to take on the biggest challenge a man can face.

The following quotation by Erwin Rommel (1891–1944) is aimed at military leaders but there is much to be learned from it for those anticipating fatherhood:

> Be an example to your men, in your duty and in private life. Never spare yourself, and let the troops see that you don't in your endurance of fatigue and privation. Always be tactful and well-mannered and teach your subordinates to do the same. Avoid excessive sharpness or harshness of voice, which usually indicates the man who has shortcomings of his own to hide.

28

SEPARATION AND DIVORCE

As a society, we are becoming less and less committed to our promises, vows, and contracts. Perhaps this is because we consider our own happiness is more important than keeping our word.

It is important to understand that if you give your word, make a vow, or sign a contract, you are expected to honour it. If you don't want to commit yourself or are unsure, don't make the commitment in the first place. It's better to face the disappointment of others before agreeing to a course of action than to face the anger caused when you fail to play your part or withdraw from a commitment.

Do not be rushed or forced into making decisions concerning your future. You may regret the consequences of bowing to such pressure for the rest of your life.

We are all human, and we all make mistakes. This is common when sharing a close relationship with another person. So when misunderstandings occur or difficulties manifest themselves, try to see things from your partner's point of view.

If it becomes clear that the relationship has no future, then consideration must be given to a formal separation. Almost certainly, one of you will be hurt emotionally. It is likely that both of you will feel the impact of the breakdown in what began as love for one another. Be dignified and decent in your discussions.

Decisions made jointly in a fair and honourable way will be of mutual benefit in the long run.

Ultimately, you must satisfy your own conscience that you did your best to save the relationship or ended it with fairness, dignity, and compassion.

No matter how angry or frustrated you feel, never resort to violence, to your partner, your children, or anyone else. By doing so, you will merely demonstrate that you regard them as nothing more than possessions. If you love them, really love them, you will not harm them. Violence to them or yourself will solve nothing and will destroy any feelings of love they have for you.

If your marriage ends and divorce becomes necessary, you will need legal advice. It will be expensive and take time. Don't expect a quick decision. The way you conduct yourself during the breakup of a marital relationship will affect what you see when you look in the mirror. Will you see a decent man? Will you be proud of yourself? If that is the case, you will deserve to find love with a new partner. If you feel ashamed at the way you've behaved, you don't really deserve another chance.

If you're a good person, love will find you. Don't give up.

29

HEALTH AND ILLNESS

Too much of most things can, and generally do, harm us.

Whilst you are young, you may not notice the effects of overindulgence; however, as you get older, your body will begin to encounter physical conditions caused by it, which can develop into seriously debilitating illnesses, perhaps death.

The following will take their toll of your health, if you continually expose yourself to them, regardless of their effects:

- Weather conditions such as the sun and extremes of heat and cold.
- Things we eat like sugar, chocolate, dairy products, meat, and salt.
- Fizzy drinks, energy drinks, and coffee.
- Alcohol, tobacco, and other drugs (including some medicines and muscle-enhancing steroids).
- Strenuous activity (or lack of activity).
- Poor living and working conditions.

As a child, your parents will have controlled your lifestyle; hopefully, they will have taught you healthy habits. As you get older, you will gain more independence. It is important that you look after your body if you want it to last a long time. Don't be drawn into what you may regard as fashionable social activities that include heavy drinking, smoking, or drug use.

Your organs form part of an incredibly complex biological engine. In a machine, if one part begins to fail, other parts come under increased pressure. Your body is no different. So you must look after all of it.

Your body will adapt to the conditions you live in. If you decide to change your lifestyle dramatically, you must understand that your physical system will need time to adapt. Consult your physician before committing yourself to extreme sports. Make changes to your lifestyle carefully.

At some stage in your life, illness or injury will almost certainly happen to you. The more you have looked after your health, the greater your chance of a rapid recovery.

Illness brings varying degrees of debilitation. Some are extremely painful to endure. Some of us have a low pain threshold, whilst others can endure severe discomfort, calmly and with stoicism. Some people have an incurable illness. Be kind to those who are in pain and discomfort or have some form of disability. Treat them as you would like to be treated if you were in the same situation. Be kind to those who deserve compassion, and do not allow others to deride or disrespect them. They need friendship and understanding as much as you do, not a pack of hyenas mocking them.

Never walk away from someone needing help because you are unsure what to do. At the very least, you can summon assistance and remain with them until help arrives, reassuring them and making them comfortable.

Finally, the mind can be damaged as easily as the body. With the body, damage and pain are generally obvious. The same cannot be said for the mind, where pain can be inflicted without any noticeable affects. So be aware that you may inflict pain, intentionally or through negligence, and do your best to protect those who may be vulnerable.

30
SOCIETY

Do you owe society anything? Well, you are a product of society. Like it or not, your development has been forged by the society you were born into and grew up in.

Whether your development has been good or bad has been beyond your control. Now, perhaps it is time to consider how you'd like to influence society in the future.

What sort of society do you want? What sort of society will you want your children to inherit?

You could, of course, do nothing. In future, you could just blame everyone else for society's shortcomings.

Alternatively, you could get involved. There are many options:

- Fundamentally, by voting in local, regional and national elections.
- At a grassroots level, in parish and town councils; school governorships; and local religious, youth, and charitable groups.
- At higher levels, in county councils, as a trustee with major trusts, regional charities and advisory boards, or as a magistrate or prison visitor.
- At the top level, in politics.

As far as voting is concerned, it is no good complaining about things that councillors and politicians make decisions about, if you can't be bothered to vote. If you were shipwrecked on a deserted island with ten other people, would you let them make all the decisions? No. Then register to vote, and most importantly, vote when it is time to do so.

If you want to improve society, you must be committed to giving it your support. Your country was built on the selfless dedication, courage, and vision of good people. Their time and effort to create the country you know today, often in the face of turmoil, was worth it, but it needs to be sustained, nurtured, and refreshed. Can you afford not to do your part?

31

SELF-HARM

Self-harm is a way for some people to cope with overwhelming emotional distress or express painful memories or situations.

It can be caused by:

- Pressure to achieve at school.
- Bullying.
- Money worries.
- Sexual, physical, or emotional abuse.
- Bereavement.
- Confusion over sexuality.
- Breakdown of a relationship.

Whilst there are professionals, such as your doctor, family members, and friends, who can provide helpful advice and support, you cannot rely entirely on others to save you from self-harm; you must ultimately learn to deal with it yourself.

Start by identifying the things that trigger the urge to hurt yourself. It may be useful to write it down each time it occurs. Once you have done this, when the trigger occurs, try to find something to distract you, to delay the urge and give you time to reduce its intensity. This could be going for a bike ride, kicking a ball about, or calling a friend, for example.

Ultimately, you must learn to accept your feelings and look after your health. Understand that none of us are perfect; learn to like yourself. You have many strengths and some weaknesses. Understanding your weaknesses is a strength.

If you know someone who is self-harming, talk to them about it, listen to them, and support them. We all need help from time to time.

32

SUICIDE

Suicide is a terrible experience which is devastating for the person who dies and those who are left behind.

Your life may be so bad that you consider the only solution is to kill yourself.

The problems you face may be physical, emotional, psychological, financial, or social. When it gets to the stage when you think *What's the point?* please bear in mind the following important points:

- There are organisations with good people out there who are able to help you. They may have experienced the same difficulties you face. They will give their time and energy for no reward, because they understand, feel your pain, and want to help.
- There are people close to you, some of whom love you, who will be devastated by your death. Not just because you have died, but because you never gave them the chance to help you, never confided in them, and never asked them to listen or understand your feelings.
- There are so many good people around you. All it takes is one to change your life and give you love, understanding, and a sense of purpose. That person will give you the

strength and determination to go on. Keep searching until you find that person. Who knows, they may be searching for you too. They may be just around the corner; never give up.

Remember you are unique. You have good qualities. You have a destiny to fulfil.

Remember too there are others who have much greater difficulties than you.

Prayer can give you peace, comfort you, and give you strength. You don't need to go to a place of worship to pray.

Those who love you, your friends, religious leaders, and charities like the Samaritans will help you in times of great distress if you give them the chance.

Don't give up your life without a bloody good fight!

I hope that these words by D. H. Lawrence (1885–1930) will give you strength, should you ever need it: "I never saw a wild thing sorry for itself. A small bird will drop frozen dead from a bough without ever having felt sorry for itself."

33

BEREAVEMENT

A sad fact of life is that we are all destined to die. As you go through life, some of those you love will die before you.

It is natural to mourn, to cry, and to experience acute sadness. The sadness will never quite go away. It will get easier to bear as time passes, but there will be times when it will re-emerge, when someone or something reminds you of the person you loved.

Death reminds us of our own mortality, so be prepared to feel very low. It will pass. It will pass more quickly if you involve yourself by supporting others who are bereaved. Funerals tend to be a celebration of a person's life; therefore, try to be positive in thoughts, words, and actions. Try not to be consumed by your own grief and self-pity, no matter how devastated you may be, because by doing so, you will ignore the needs of others experiencing the same sense of loss.

Emotional pain is far more difficult to treat than physical injury. Bereavement counselling is available through your doctor. So if you suffer from depression due to bereavement, act quickly.

Ultimately, you will be left with your own thoughts. Try to honour the memory of the person you have lost by living a decent, fruitful, and happy life. You only get one chance. Live the sort of life that results in people mourning you when it ends.

The dead rarely have the chance to leave a message for mourners at their funeral. Given the opportunity to do so, they might use the following words to give the bereaved comfort:

An Old Irish Blessing

May the road rise up to meet you.
May the wind always be at your back.
May the sun shine warm upon your face,
and rains fall softly on your fields.
And until we meet again,
May God hold you in the palm of His hand.

34

DEATH

If you are lucky, you will have the chance to prepare for death. Many people die without warning, losing any chance to ensure nothing is left undone or unsaid.

Most are unprepared for death, but it is perhaps worth considering what regrets you might have when death approaches.

We are all human; therefore, we will have made mistakes in our lifetime. Naturally, we will all have regrets of some sort. We may have hurt others, for example. To be free of regrets, you must live your life without hurting anyone, physically or emotionally. This takes strength and goodness of character, because we all have a tendency towards selfishness and self-indulgence.

If you have lived a full and decent life, when death is near, you can face it with a clear conscience, knowing you have done your best. This will ease the terrible sadness that comes with the understanding that your life is about to end.

35

PETS

Be under no illusion: If you have a pet, you are totally responsible for its health and well-being.

Pets cannot tell you if they are unhappy or unwell. It is up to you to learn the signs that your pet displays in order to assess their condition.

Some creatures are easy to manage and monitor; others are not. It is important, therefore, that you research the creature you plan to own before taking responsibility for it. You must also ensure that you have the time and energy to look after it. This will ensure you know what your duty is in respect of its care.

Abuse and ill-treatment of any form of animal is a most cowardly and inhuman act. They cannot understand cruelty inflicted on them through ignorance, intolerance, or sheer brutality. If you own a pet, it will rely on you; after all, you are supposed to have the knowledge, intelligence, and resources that it does not.

If you cannot look after it, don't abandon it, kill it, or abuse it. There are plenty of charitable organisations that will take it off your hands and care for it properly.

Animals don't understand honour and dignity, but you should. If you are cruel to an animal, you will never forget it and bear the shame always.

If you can't understand this message, don't have a pet.

36

SPORT

There is a wide variety of sport available to you.

Some sports require physical strength, agility, and courage. Some do not require muscles but do require dexterity and concentration. There are sports which rely on coordinated teamwork and others that are entirely for individuals.

Most of us are better at some than others.

There are blind skiers, wheelchair tennis players, and legless runners who consider their handicaps challenges to be overcome. They set us all a good example of what sport is all about.

Sport is to be enjoyed, so have a go at all the sports you get the opportunity to do. Don't give up. There is a sport that will suit you. You may not be great at it, but you will benefit from taking part because doing so will be good for you physically, by improving your fitness, and mentally, by allowing you to concentrate on something other than the routine endeavours of everyday life.

Sport will also give you the opportunity to make new friends.

Have a go.

The following pages give details of some notable sporting achievements.

OLYMPIC GAMES MALE MARATHON WINNERS

Year	Runner	Nationality	Time
490 BC	Pheidippides	Greek	
1896	Spiridon Louis	Greek	2:58:50
1900	Michel Théato	Luxembourger	2:59:45
1904	Thomas Hicks	American	3:28:53
1906	William Sherring	Canadian	2:51:23.6
1908	John Hayes	American	2:55:18.4
1912	Kenneth McArthur	South African	2:36:54.8

1914–1918: The First World War

Year	Runner	Nationality	Time
1920	Hannes Kolehmainen	Finnish	2:32:35.8
1924	Albin Stenroos	Finnish	2:41:22.6
1928	Boughera El Ouafi	Algerian	2:32:57.0
1932	Juan Carlos Zabala	Argentinian	2:31:36.0
1936	Kee-Chung Sohn	Korean	2:29:19.2

1939–1945: The Second World War

Year	Runner	Nationality	Time
1948	Delfo Cabrera	Argentinian	2:34:51:6
1952	Emil Zátopek	Czechoslovakian	2:23:03.2
1956	Alain Mimoun	Algerian	2:25:00.0

1960	Abebe Bikila	Ethiopian	2:15:16.2
1964	Abebe Bikila	Ethiopian	2:12:11.2
1968	Mamo Wolde	Ethiopian	2:20:26.4
1972	Frank Shorter	American	2:12:19.8
1976	Waldermar Cierpinski	East German	2:09:55
1980	Waldermar Cierpinski	East German	2:11:03
1984	Carlos Lopez	Portuguese	2:09:21
1988	Gelindo Bordin	Italian	2:10:32
1992	Hwang Yeong-Jo	Korean	2:13:23
1996	Josia Thugwane	South African	2:12:36
2000	Gezahegne Abera	Ethiopian	2:10:11
2004	Stefano Baldini	Italian	2:10:55
2008	Samuel Kamau	Kenyan	2:06:32
2012	Stephen Kiprotich	Ugandan	2:08:01
2016	Eliud Kipchoge Rotich	Kenyan	2:08:44

FOOTBALL WORLD CUP FINAL RESULTS

*Asterisks denote the times they have won

Year	Winner	Runner-up	Score
1930	Uruguay*	Argentina	4–2
1934	Italy*	Czechoslovakia	2–1
1938	Italy**	Hungary	4–2

1939–1945: The Second World War

Year	Winner	Runner-up	Score
1950	Uruguay**	Brazil	2–1
1954	West Germany*	Hungary	3–2
1958	Brazil*	Sweden	5–2
1962	Brazil**	Czechoslovakia	3–1
1966	England*	West Germany	4–2
1970	Brazil***	Italy	4–1
1974	West Germany**	Netherlands	2–1
1978	Argentina*	Netherlands	3–1
1982	Italy***	West Germany	3–1
1986	Argentina**	West Germany	3–2
1990	West Germany***	Argentina	1–0
1994	Brazil****	Italy	3–2 (pen)
1998	France*	Brazil	3–0

2002	Brazil*****	Germany	2–0
2006	Italy****	France	5–3 (pen)
2010	Spain*	Netherlands	1–0
2014	Germany****	Argentina	1–0
2018	France**	Croatia	4–2

37

FINALLY

During your life, you will be dealt many cards. You will rarely have the chance to choose them or select the moment you receive or determine how you play them. Some will be useful and easy to play; others will be difficult, often giving you little or no options. You can only play them to the best of your ability. It is important that you do so. Only by doing your best will you find any degree of satisfaction and self-respect. When the going gets tough, it might be easy to give in to human frailty, and you can be forgiven for doing so; however, you will know if you have done less than you could have and will gain no comfort from it. Don't be afraid; take advice from someone you trust, but don't give up. Never give up. (With sincere thanks to JC McColl).

Whatever you experience in life, be proud of what you achieve. Whatever direction you choose now is entirely dependent on your needs, aspirations, and desires. Choose wisely. Take your time when selecting your path; it will be time well spent and seldom wasted. You are young and resilient, and the world is out there, waiting for your contribution to its development and prosperity. Take heart, and be strong. The world needs the young.

Be true to yourself. Don't tolerate cruelty. Love, but don't expect too much of it. Do what you know is right, and take courage in what you are doing. Know your limitations, but don't be restricted by them. Understand that fear is normal, but you can overcome it.

Most of us live average lives. Those who are famous, gifted, or fortunate will die eventually as will you. Don't envy them. Identify what you are good at, pursue it, and be truly satisfied with the life you have created for yourself.

If you want to be a carpenter, be a good carpenter.
If you want to be a husband, be a good husband.
If you want to be a father, be a good father.
If you want to be a man, be a good man.
If you do that, you will be a legend. Don't give up.

The following poem, written in 1910 by Rudyard Kipling (1865–1936), is a fitting end to this book. I wish you good luck in all you do.

If

If you can keep your head when all about you
Are losing theirs and blaming it on you,
If you can trust yourself when all men doubt you,
But make allowance for their doubt too;
If you can wait and not be tired by waiting,
Or being lied about, don't deal in lies,
Or being hated, don't give way to hating,
And yet don't look too good, nor talk too wise:
If you can dream—and not make dreams your master;
If you can think—and not make thoughts your aim;
If you can meet with Triumph and Disaster
And treat those two impostors just the same;
If you can bear to hear the truth you've spoken
Twisted by knaves to make a trap for fools,
Or watch the things you gave your life to, broken,
And stoop and build 'em up with worn-out tools:

A Guide To Life For Young Men Aged 13+

If you can make one heap of all your winnings
   And risk it on one turn of pitch-and-toss,
And lose, and start again at your beginnings
   And never breathe a word about your loss;
If you can force your heart and nerve and sinew
   To serve your turn long after they are gone,
And so hold on when there is nothing in you
Except the Will which says to them: "Hold on!"

If you can talk with crowds and keep your virtue,
Or walk with Kings—nor lose the common touch,
   if neither foes nor loving friends can hurt you,
If all men count with you, but none too much;
   If you can fill the unforgiving minute
   With sixty seconds' worth of distance run,
Yours is the Earth and everything that's in it,
And—which is more—you'll be a man, my son!

Lightning Source UK Ltd.
Milton Keynes UK
UKHW042213080320
359884UK00019B/180

9 781982 281380